這本書將幫助您準備為美國公民測試

U.S. Citizenship Test
Chinese · English · 中文· 英文
100 Bilingual Questions and Answers

新版公民入籍歸化考試的100道考題與答案

D1715885

U.S. Citizenship Test
Chinese · English · 中文· 英文
100 Bilingual Questions and Answers

Published by Lakewood Publishing
an imprint of Learning Visions
1710 Moorpark Rd., Suite #213
Thousand Oaks, CA 91362

ISBN: 978-1-936583-05-8 (paperback)
1. Citizenship, United States, America, U.S. 2. naturalization,
citizenship
3. immigration, citizenship test, new test
4 Chinese – language 5. Mandarin - language 6. English - language
7. bilingual – language
9. United States – civics, government
9. United States – USCIS new test October 2008
I. Citizenship, American   II. Title

U.S. Citizenship Test

Chinese · English · 中文 · 英文

100 Bilingual Questions and Answers

新版公民入籍歸化考試的100道考題與答案

J.S. Aaron

Available Online:

Translation Software:

www.googletranslate.com
www.babelfish.com

(These can be helpful, but they do not give perfect translations. They are best used with single words or simple sentences.)

Also, you can see a USCIS Sample Citizenship Interview online at:

www.welcomeesl.com
(Welcome ESL)
or
www.uscis.gov
United States Citizenship and Immigration Services

Also Available from Lakewood Publishing

*Learn About the United States: Quick Civics Lessons for the New NaturalizationTest
ISBN: 978-1-936583-01-0 (hardback)
ISBN: 978-0-9793538-1-9 (paperback)
ISBN 978-0-9793538-9-5 (digital/ebook)

*U.S. Citizenship Test Practice (2011-2012): How to Prepare for the United States Citizenship Test and Interview—and Pass
ISBN: 978-1-936583-14-0

U.S. Citizenship Test Questions in 5 Languages--English, Spanish, Chinese, Tagalog and Vietnamese
English -Español - 中英 - Tagalog - tiếng Việt
ISBN: 978-1-936583-11-9   (hardback)

*U.S. Citizenship Test (English edition): 100 Questions and Answers Includes a Flash Card Format for Easy Practice
ISBN: 978-1-936583-04-1

*U.S.Citizenship Test (English and Spanish - Español y Inglés) **100 Bilingual Questions and Answers** 100 Preguntas y respuestas del exámen de ciudadanía (2011-2012)
ISBN: 978-1-936583-07-2

US Citizenship Test (Chinese-English-中英) **100 Bilingual Questions and Answers**
新版公民入籍歸化考試的100道考題與答案
ISBN: 978-1-936583-05-8

U.S. Citizenship Test: 100 Bilingual Questions and Answers
(Filipino – Tagalog – Ingles – English)   **100 Katanungan at Sagot para sa Iksamen sa U.S. Naturalisasyon**
ISBN: : 978-1-936583-09-6

U.S. Citizenship Test: 100 Bilingual Questions and Answers
(Vietnamese - English - tiếng Việt - tiếng Anh) **100 câu hỏi và câu trả lời để chuẩn bị cho kỹ thi quốc tich Mỹ**
ISBN: 978-0-936583-12-6

目錄 / Table of Contents

中文
Chinese

English
英文

Important:
Many questions have more than one correct answer. For your test, you usually only need to know one answer. If you need to know more than one answer, the question will say how many answers you need to know.

中文
Chinese

新版公民入籍歸化考試的100道考題與答案

簡介
(USCIS)

新版公民入籍歸化考試 (歷史與政府) 的考題

以下所列出的為新版公民 (歷史與政府) 入籍歸化考試的100道考題與答案.

凡是於2008年10月1日之後, 填寫 N-400 公民入籍申請表格的申請人 均需要仔細研讀這100道考題與答案. 公民入籍歸化考試採用口試方式.

由美國移民局官員自這100道題庫中提出至多10題問題詢問申請人.

申請人必需至少答對10題中的6題, 才能通過公民入籍歸化考試.

雖然美國移民局明白這100道考題可能會有額外的正確答案,但是我們建議申請人採用本題庫提供的解答來答覆公民入籍歸化口試.

如果您已年滿65歲或65歲以上, 並且已經持有美國合法永久居留權 (俗稱綠卡) 20年或更久,
您只需要研
讀標示有星號 (*) 的考題.

美國政府

A: 美國民主原則

1. 美國的最高法律是什麼？

   - 憲法

2. 憲法的作用是什麼？

   - 建立政府體制
   - 定義政府
   - 保護美國人的基本權利

3. 憲法的前三個字說明自治的概念. 這三個字是什麼？

   - 我們人民

4. 什麼是修正案？

   - （憲法的）更正
   - （憲法的）補充

5. 憲法的前十項修正案稱為什麼？

   - 權利法案

6. 列舉憲法第一條修正案中的一項權利或自由 ?*

   - 言論自由
   - 宗教自由
   - 集會結社的自由
   - 出版自由
   - 向政府請願的自由

7. 憲法有幾條修正案？

   - 二十七（27）條

8. 「獨立宣言」的作用是什麼？

   - 宣佈美國（脫離英國而）獨立
   - 宣告美國（脫離英國而）獨立
   - 表示美國（脫離英國而）獨立

9. 列舉「獨立宣言」中的兩項權利 ？

   - 生命（的權利）
   - 自由（的權利）
   - 追求幸福（的權利）

10. 什麼是宗教自由？

    - 你可以信仰任何宗教，也可以不信仰任何宗教.

8

11. 美國的經濟制度是什麼？

- 資本主義經濟
- 市場經濟

12. 「法治」是什麼？

- 人人都應遵守法律．
- 領導人必須遵守法律．
- 政府必須遵守法律．
- 沒有任何人在法律之上．

美國歷史

B: 政治體制

13. 列舉政府體制的一個分支或部門．*

- 國會
- 立法部門
- 總統
- 行政部門
- 法院
- 司法部門

14. 什麼防止一個政府分支變得過於強大？

- 制衡
- 權力分立

15. 誰負責行政部門？

   ▪ 總統

16. 誰制定聯邦法律？

   ▪ 國會
   ▪ 參議院及眾議院
   ▪ （美國或國家）立法部門

17. 美國國會由哪兩個部分組成？＊

   ▪ 參議院與眾議院

18. 美國參議員有幾位？

   ▪ 一百（100）位

19. 我們選出的美國參議員任職多少年？

   ▪ 六（6）年

20. 您所在州的現任一位美國參議員的名字是什麼？＊

   ▪ 答案依所在州不同而異．［住在哥倫比亞特區和美國領
   土的居民可答：哥倫比亞特區當地
   （或應試居民所在領地）　沒有美國參議員．］

21. 眾議院中有投票權的眾議員有幾位?

- 四百三十五（435）位

22. 我們選出的美國眾議員任職多少年?

- 兩（2）年

23. 列舉您所在選區的美國眾議員的名字．

- 答案依所在州不同而異
．〔住在沒有投票權的美國領地當地代表或專員之應試者可以說明當地代表或專員的姓名．
說明自己選區沒有國會（投票）代表也是可接受的答案．〕

24. 美國參議員代表何人?

- 其所在州的所有人民

25. 為什麼有些州的眾議員人數比其他州多?

- （由於）該州的人口
- （由於）該州有更多人口
- （由於）該州的人口比其他州多

26. 我們選出的總統任職多少年?

- 四（4）年

11

27. 我們在哪一個月選總統？＊

   ▪ 十一月

28. 現任美國總統的名字是什麼？＊

   ▪ Barack Obama
   ▪ Obama

29. 現任美國副總統的名字是什麼？

   ▪ Joseph R. Biden, Jr.
   ▪ Joe Biden
   ▪ Biden

30. 如果總統不能視事，則由誰成為總統？

   ▪ 副總統

31. 如果總統和副總統都不能視事，則由誰成為總統？

   ▪ 眾議院議長

32. 誰是三軍統帥？

   ▪ 總統

12

33. 誰簽署法案使之成為法律？

   - 總統

34. 誰否決法案？

   - 總統

35. 總統的內閣做什麼事？

   - 向總統提出建議

36. <u>兩個</u>內閣級別的職位是什麼？

   - 農業部長　　　　　- 財政部長
   - 商務部長　　　　　- 退伍軍人事務部長
   - 國防部長　　　　　- 司法部長
   - 教育部長　　　　　- 副總統
   - 能源部長
   - 健康與人類服務部長
   - 國土安全部長
   - 住宅與都市發展部長
   - 內政部長
   - 勞工部長
   - 國務卿
   - 交通部長

37. 司法部門做什麼？

- 審查法律
- 解釋法律
- 解決爭議（意見不一致）
- 決定某一法律是否牴觸憲法

38. 美國最高法院是什麼？

- 聯邦最高法院

39. 最高法院有幾位大法官？

- 九（9）位

40. 現任聯邦首席大法官是誰？

- 約翰 • 羅伯茲（小約翰 G. 羅伯茲）

41. 根據我國憲法，有些權力屬於聯邦政府．
聯邦政府的一項權力是什麼？

- 印製鈔票
- 宣戰
- 創立軍隊
- 簽訂條約

42. 根據我國憲法，有些權力屬於州政府.
州政府的一項權力是什麼？

- 提供教育
- 提供保護（警員）
- 提供安全（消防局）
- 提供駕駛執照
- 批准區劃與土地使用

43. 您居住州的現任州長是誰？

- 答案依居住州不同而異. ［哥倫比亞特區的居民應回
答：我們沒有州長.］

44. 您居住州的首府是哪裡？ *

- 答案依居住州不同而異. ［哥倫比亞特區居民應回答哥
倫比亞特區不是一個州，沒有首府. 美國領地居民應回答
居住領地的首府.］

45. 美國當今兩大政黨為何？ *

- 民主黨與共和黨

46. 現任總統屬於哪個政黨？

- 民主黨

47. 現任國會眾議院議長的名字是什麼？

- （南茜）波洛西

C: 權利與責任

48. 憲法中有四個關於誰可以投票的修正案. 試舉一個. _

- 十八 *(18)* 歲以上的公民（可以投票）.
- 您投票不必繳錢（繳投票稅）.
- 任何公民都可以投票（男性與女性都可以投票）.
- 任何種族的男性公民（都可以投票）.

49. 列舉一項美國公民才有的責任？ *

- 當陪審員
- 在聯邦選舉中投票

50. 列舉一項美國公民才享有的權利.

- 在聯邦選舉中投票的權利
- 競選公職的權利

51. 每一個住在美國的人享有的兩項權利是什麼？

   ▪ 表達自由
   ▪ 言論自由
   ▪ 集會結社的自由
   ▪ 向政府請願的自由
   ▪ 宗教崇拜的自由
   ▪ 持有武器的自由

52. 當我們宣誓效忠時．是向什麼表達忠誠？

   ▪ 美利堅合眾國
   ▪ 國旗

53. 當您成為美國公民時做出的一項承諾是什麼？

   ▪ 放棄效忠其他國家
   ▪ 護衛美國的憲法及法律
   ▪ 遵守美國的法律
   ▪ （必要時）加入美國軍隊
   ▪ （必要時）為國效勞（為國做重要工作）
   ▪ 效忠美國

54. 美國公民必須幾歲才能投票選舉總統？ *

   ▪ 十八（18）歲以上

55. 美國人參與民主政治的兩種方法是什麼？

- 投票
- 加入政黨
- 協助競選活動
- 加入公民團體
- 加入社區團體
- 向民選官員提供自己對某項議題的意見
- 撥電給參議員和眾議員
- 公開支持或反對某個議題或政策
- 競選公職
- 向報社投函

56. 寄送聯邦所得稅表的截止日期是哪一天？*

- （每年的）4月15日

57. 所有男性到了哪個年齡必須註冊「兵役登記」？

- 十八（18）歲
- 十八（18）歲至二十六（26）歲之間

美國歷史

A: 殖民期與獨立

58. 殖民者當初到美國的一項理由是什麼？

- 自由
- 政治自由
- 宗教自由
- 經濟機會
- 從事宗教活動
- 逃避迫害

59. 歐洲人抵達美國之前，誰已經居住在美國？

- 美國印地安人
- 美國原住民

60. 哪一群人被帶到美國並被販賣為奴？

- 非洲人
- 來自非洲的人

61. 殖民者為何與英國作戰？

- 因為高額捐稅（只繳稅，沒有代表權）
- 因為英國軍隊住在他們的住宅內（寄宿，宿營）
- 因為他們沒有自治權

62. 「獨立宣言」是誰寫的？

   ▪ （湯瑪士）傑佛遜

63. 「獨立宣言」是何時通過採用的？

   ▪ **1776** 年**7**月**4**日

64. 美國原先有13個州．請列舉其中三個州．

   ▪ 新罕布夏
   ▪ 麻薩諸塞
   ▪ 羅德島
   ▪ 康乃狄克
   ▪ 紐約
   ▪ 紐澤西
   ▪ 賓夕法尼亞
   ▪ 德拉瓦
   ▪ 馬裏蘭
   ▪ 維吉尼亞
   ▪ 北卡羅萊納
   ▪ 南卡羅萊納
   ▪ 喬治亞

65. 制憲會議達成了什麼事？

   ▪ 擬定憲法．
   ▪ 開國諸賢擬定了憲法．

66. 憲法是何時擬定的？

- **1787**年

67. 《聯邦論》支持美國憲法的通過.
請列舉一名《聯邦論》的作者.

- （詹姆士）麥迪森
- （亞歷山大）漢米爾頓
- （約翰）傑伊
-   普布利烏斯

68. 班哲明 •　富蘭克林著稱的一項事蹟是什麼？

- 美國外交官
- 制憲會議年紀最長的成員
- 美國第一任郵政總局局長
- 《窮人理查年鑑》的作者
- 開辦第一個免費圖書館

69. 誰是「美國國父」？

- （喬治）華盛頓

George Washington

70. 誰是第一任總統？*

- （喬治）華盛頓

B：1800年代

71. 美國在1803年向法國購買哪塊領地？

- 路易士安納領地
- 路易士安納

72. 列舉一場美國在1800年代參與的戰爭 。

- 1812年戰爭
- 美墨戰爭
- 內戰
- 美國與西班牙戰爭

73. 請說出美國南方與北方之間戰爭的名稱 .

- 內戰
- 州際戰爭

74. 列舉一項導致內戰的問題.

- 奴隸制度
- 經濟原因
- 各州的權利

75. 亞伯拉罕 ・ 林肯的一項重要事蹟是什麼？*

- 解放奴隸（《解放宣言》）
- 拯救（保留）聯盟
- 在內戰期間引領美國

76.《解放宣言》達成了什麼？

- 解放了奴隸
- 解放了聯邦制下的奴隸
- 解放了聯邦各州的奴隸
- 解放了南方大部分州的奴隸

77. 蘇珊B. 安東尼的事蹟是什麼？

- 為女權奮鬥
- 為民權奮鬥

C： 美國近代史與其他重要的歷史資料

78. 列舉一場美國在1900年代參與的戰爭. *

- 第一次世界大戰
- 第二次世界大戰
- 朝鮮戰爭
- 越戰
- （波斯灣）海灣戰爭

79. 第一次世界大戰期間的美國總統是誰？

   ▪ （伍德羅）威爾遜

Abraham Lincoln

80. 美國經濟大蕭條和第二次世界大戰期間的總統是誰？

   ▪ （富蘭克林）羅斯福

81. 美國在第二次世界大戰與哪些國家作戰？

   ▪ 日本、德國、義大利

82. 艾森豪在當總統以前是將軍．他曾參加哪一場戰爭？

   ▪ 第二次世界大戰

83. 在冷戰期間，美國的主要顧慮是什麼？

   ▪ 共產主義

84. 哪項運動試圖結束種族歧視？

- 民權（運動）

85. 小馬丁‧ 路德‧ 金的事蹟是什麼？*

- 為民權奮鬥
- 為所有美國人爭取平等

86. 美國在2001年9月11日發生了什麼重大事件？

- 恐怖份子攻擊美國．

87. 列舉一個美國印地安人部族．
[USCIS主考官將有聯邦承認的美國印地安人部族清單．]

- 賀皮
- 伊努特
- 切洛基
- 納瓦荷
- 蘇
- 齊普瓦
- 喬克陶
- 布耶布洛
- 阿帕契
- 伊洛奎斯
- 庫瑞克
- 佈雷克非特
- 賽米諾利
- 夏安

- 拉科塔
- 克洛
- 泰頓
- 阿拉瓦克
- 蕭尼
- 莫希根
- 休倫
- 歐尼達

綜合公民（歸化試題）

A：地理

88. 列舉美國最長的兩條河中的一條．

- 密蘇裏（河）
- 密西西比（河）

89. 美國西岸瀕臨什麼海洋？

- 太平洋

90. 美國東岸瀕臨什麼海洋？

- 大西洋

91. 列舉一個美國領地．

- 波多黎各
- 美屬維京群島
- 美屬薩摩亞
- 北馬裏亞納群島
- 關島

92. 列舉一個與加拿大毗連的州．

- 緬因
- 明尼蘇達
- 新罕布夏
- 北達科他
- 佛蒙特
- 蒙大拿
- 紐約
- 愛達荷
- 賓夕法尼亞
- 華盛頓
- 俄亥俄
- 阿拉斯加
- 密西根

93. 列舉一個與墨西哥毗連的州．

- 加利福尼亞
- 亞利桑那
- 新墨西哥
- 德克薩斯

94. 美國的首都在哪裡？＊

- 華盛頓哥倫比亞特區

95. 自由女神像在哪裡？＊

- 紐約（港）
- 自由島
  ［回答紐澤西、紐約市附近、哈德遜河上也可以接受］

B：標誌

96. 國旗上為什麼有十三個條紋？

- 因為當初有十三個殖民地
- 因為條紋代表當初的殖民地

97. 國旗上為什麼有五十顆星星？＊

- 因為一個州有一顆星
- 因為一顆星代表一個州
- 因為有五十個州

98. 美國國歌的名稱是什麼？

- 星條旗之歌

C：國定假日

99. 我們在哪一天慶祝獨立紀念日？＊

- 7月4日

28

100. 列舉<u>兩個</u>美國的國定假日 。

- 新年
- 馬丁路德金的生日
- 總統日
- 國殤日
- 美國國慶日
- 勞動節
- 哥倫布日
- 退伍軍人節
- 感恩節
- 聖誕節

美國國慶日

65/20

如果您已年滿65歲或65歲以上，並且已經持有美國合法永久
居留權(俗稱綠卡)20年或更久，則您只需要研讀標示有星號

＊ 的考題。

65/20
(USCIS)

如果您已年滿65歲或65歲以上,
並且已經持有美國合法永久居留權（俗稱綠卡）20年或更久,
您只需要研讀標示有星號（*）的考題.

6.　列舉憲法第一條修正案中的一項權利或自由 ?*

- 言論自由
- 宗教自由
- 集會結社的自由
- 出版自由
- 向政府請願的自由

11.　美國的經濟制度是什麼？

- 資本主義經濟
- 市場經濟

B：政治體制

13.　列舉政府體制的一個分支或部門 .*

- 國會
- 立法部門
- 總統
- 行政部門
- 法院
- 司法部門

17. 美國國會由哪兩個部分組成？*

   ▪ 參議院與眾議院

20. 您所在州的現任一位美國參議員的名字是什麼？*

   ▪ 答案依所在州不同而異．［住在哥倫比亞特區和美國領
   土的居民可答:哥倫比亞特區當地
   （或應試居民所在領地）　沒有美國參議員．］

27. 我們在哪一個月選總統？*

   ▪ 十一月

28. 現任美國總統的名字是什麼？*

   ▪ Barack Obama
   ▪ Obama

44. 您居住州的首府是哪裡？*

   ▪ 答案依居住州不同而異．［哥倫比亞特區居民應回答哥
   倫比亞特區不是一個州，沒有首府．美國領地居民應回答
   居住領地的首府．］

45. 美國當今兩大政黨為何？＊

- 民主黨與共和黨

C：權利與責任

49. 列舉一項美國公民才有的責任？＊

- 當陪審員
- 在聯邦選舉中投票

54. 美國公民必須幾歲才能投票選舉總統？＊

- 十八（18）歲以上

56. 寄送聯邦所得稅表的截止日期是哪一天？＊

- （每年的）4月15日

美國歷史

70. 誰是第一任總統？＊

- （喬治）華盛頓

B：1800年代

75. 亞伯拉罕 •　林肯的一項重要事蹟是什麼？ ＊

- 解放奴隸（《解放宣言》）
- 拯救（保留）聯盟
- 在內戰期間引領美國

C：美國近代史與其他重要的歷史資料

78. 列舉一場美國在1900年代參與的戰爭.　＊

- 第一次世界大戰
- 第二次世界大戰
- 朝鮮戰爭
- 越戰
- （波斯灣）海灣戰爭

85. 小馬丁•　路德 •　金的事蹟是什麼？ ＊

- 為民權奮鬥
- 為所有美國人爭取平等

94. 美國的首都在哪裡？ ＊

- 華盛頓哥倫比亞特區

95. 自由女神像在哪裡？＊

- 紐約（港）
- 自由島
  ［回答紐澤西、紐約市附近、哈德遜河上也可以接受］

B：標誌

97. 國旗上為什麼有五十顆星星？＊

- 因為一個州有一顆星
- 因為一顆星代表一個州
- 因為有五十個州

99. 我們在哪一天慶祝獨立紀念日？＊

- 7月4日

English

100 Civics Questions and Answers for the Citizenship-Naturalization Test

Introduction
(USCIS-INS)

The 100 civics (history and government) questions and answers for the redesigned (new) naturalization test are listed below.

If you filed your Application for Naturalization, Form N-400, on or after October 1, 2008, you will be asked questions from this list. The civics test is an oral test and the USCIS Officer will ask you up to 10 of the 100 civics questions below.

You must answer 6 out of 10 questions correctly to pass the civics portion of the naturalization test. You will also be asked other oral questions about information on your N-400 form. Know it well.

Although USCIS knows that there may be other correct answers to the 100 civics questions below, you are encouraged to answer using the answers provided below.

Remember: Some questions will list more than one correct answer. Usually, you only need to know ONE answer.

If you need to know more than one answer, the question will tell you to know more than one answer. Otherwise, you only need to know one of the answers on the list.

Note: *If you are 65 years old or older and have been a legal permanent resident of the United States for 20 or more years, you only need to know the questions that are marked with an asterisk. (*) .

American Government

A: Principles of American Democracy

1. What is the supreme law of the land?

the Constitution

2. What does the Constitution do?

- sets up the government
- defines the government
- protects basic rights of Americans

3. The idea of self-government is in the first three words of the Constitution. What are these words?

We the People

4. What is an amendment?

- a change (to the Constitution)
- an addition (to the Constitution)

5. What do we call the first ten amendments to the Constitution?

the Bill of Rights

6. What is one right or freedom from the First Amendment?*

- speech
- religion
- assembly
- press
- petition the government

7. How many amendments does the Constitution have?

twenty-seven (27)

8. What did the Declaration of Independence do?

- announced our independence (from Great Britain)
- declared our independence (from Great Britain)
- said that the United States is free (from Great Britain)

9. What are two rights in the Declaration of Independence?

- life
- liberty
- pursuit of happiness

10. What is freedom of religion?

You can practice any religion, or not practice (have) a religion.

11. What is the economic system in the United States?*

- capitalist economy
- market economy

12. What is the "rule of law"?

- Everyone must follow the law.
- Leaders must obey the law.
- Government must obey the law.
- No one is above the law.

B: System of Government

13. Name one branch or part of the government.*

- Congress
- legislative
- President
- executive
- the courts
- judicial

14. What stops one branch of government from becoming too powerful?

    - checks and balances
    - separation of powers

15. Who is in charge of the executive branch?

    the President

16. Who makes federal laws?

    - Congress
    -Senate and House (of Representatives)
    - (U.S. or national) legislature

17. What are the two parts of the U.S. Congress?*

    the Senate and House (of Representatives)

18. How many U.S. Senators are there?

    one hundred (100)

19. We elect a U.S. Senator for how many years?

    six (6)

20. Who is one of your state's U.S. Senators now?*

■ Answers will be different for each state. Check the internet **www.senate.gov** for the current names in your state. [District of Columbia residents and residents of U.S. territories should answer that D.C. (or the territory where the applicant lives) has no U.S. Senators.]

21. The House of Representatives has how many voting members?

four hundred thirty-five (435)

22. We elect a U.S. Representative for how many years?

two (2)

23. Name your U.S. Representative.

■ Answers will be different for each area. See the website: www.house.gov for the newest names. [Residents of territories with non-voting Delegates or Resident Commissioners may provide the name of that Delegate or Commissioner. Also acceptable is any statement that the territory has no (voting) Representatives in Congress.]

24. Who does a U.S. Senator represent?

all people of the state

25. Why do some states have more Representatives than other states?

- (because of) the state's population
- (because) they have more people
- (because) some states have more people

26. We elect a President for how many years?

four (4)

27. In what month do we vote for President?*

November

28. What is the name of the President of the United States now?*

- Barack Obama
- Obama

29. What is the name of the Vice President of the United States now?

- Joseph R. Biden, Jr.
- Joe Biden
- Biden

30. If the President can no longer serve, who becomes President?

the Vice President

31. If both the President and the Vice President can no longer serve, who becomes President?

the Speaker of the House

32. Who is the Commander in Chief of the military?

the President

33. Who signs bills to become laws?

the President

34. Who vetoes bills?

the President

35. What does the President's Cabinet do?

advises the President

36. What are two Cabinet-level positions?

- Vice President
- Attorney General
- Secretary of Agriculture
- Secretary of Commerce
- Secretary of Defense
- Secretary of Education
- Secretary of Energy
- Secretary of Health and Human Services
- Secretary of Homeland Security
- Secretary of Housing and Urban Development
- Secretary of the Interior
- Secretary of Labor
- Secretary of State
- Secretary of Transportation
- Secretary of the Treasury
- Secretary of Veterans Affairs

37. What does the judicial branch do?

- reviews laws
- explains laws
- resolves disputes (disagreements)
- decides if a law goes against the Constitution

38. What is the highest court in the United States?

the Supreme Court

39. How many justices are on the Supreme Court?

    nine (9)

40. Who is the Chief Justice of the United States now?

    John Roberts (John G. Roberts, Jr.)

41. Under our Constitution, some powers belong to the federal government. What is one power of the federal government?

    - to print money
    - to declare war
    - to create an army
    - to make treaties

42. Under our Constitution, some powers belong to the states. What is one power of the states?

    - provide schooling and education
    - provide protection (police)
    - provide safety (fire departments)
    - give a driver's license
    - approve zoning and land use

43. Who is the Governor of your state now?
    ▪ Answers will be different for each state.
    [District of Columbia residents should answer
    that D.C. does not have a Governor.]

44. What is the capital of your state?*

The States and the State Capitals

Alabama - Montgomery
Alaska - Juneau
Arizona - Phoenix
Arkansas - Little Rock
California - Sacramento
Colorado - Denver
Connecticut - Hartford
Delaware - Dover
Florida - Tallahassee
Georgia - Atlanta
Hawaii - Honolulu
Idaho - Boise
Illinois - Springfield
Indiana - Indianapolis
Iowa - Des Moines
Kansas - Topeka
Kentucky - Frankfort
Louisiana - Baton Rouge
Maine - Augusta
Maryland - Annapolis
Massachusetts - Boston
Michigan - Lansing
Minnesota - St. Paul
Mississippi - Jackson
Missouri - Jefferson City
Montana - Helena

Nebraska - Lincoln
Nevada - Carson City
New Hampshire - Concord
New Jersey - Trenton
New Mexico - Santa Fe
New York - Albany
North Carolina - Raleigh
North Dakota - Bismarck
Ohio - Columbus
Oklahoma - Oklahoma City
Oregon - Salem
Pennsylvania - Harrisburg
Rhode Island - Providence
South Carolina - Columbia
South Dakota - Pierre
Tennessee - Nashville
Texas - Austin
Utah - Salt Lake City
Vermont - Montpelier
Virginia - Richmond
Washington - Olympia
West Virginia - Charleston
Wisconsin - Madison
Wyoming - Cheyenne

[District of Columbia residents should answer that D.C. is not a state and does not have a capital. Residents of U.S. territories should name the capital of the territory.]

45. What are the two major political parties in the United States?*

Democratic and Republican

46. What is the political party of the President now?

Democratic (Party)

47. What is the name of the Speaker of the House of Representatives now?

(John) Boehner

C: Rights and Responsibilities

48. There are four amendments to the Constitution about who can vote. Describe one of them.

- Citizens eighteen (18) and older (can vote).
- You don't have to pay (a poll tax) to vote.
- Any citizen can vote. (Women and men can vote.)
- A male citizen of any race (can vote).

49. What is one responsibility that is only for United States citizens?*

    (1) serve on a jury;
    (2) vote in a federal election

50. Name one right only for United States citizens.

    - vote in a federal election
    - run for federal office

51. What are <u>two</u> rights of everyone living in the United States?

- freedom of expression   - freedom of worship
- freedom of speech   - the right to bear arms
- freedom of assembly
- freedom to petition the government

52. What do we show loyalty to when we say the Pledge of Allegiance?

    - the United States
    - the flag

53. What is one promise you make when you become a United States citizen?

- give up loyalty to other countries
- defend the Constitution and laws of the United States
- obey the laws of the United States
- serve in the U.S. military (if needed)
- serve (do important work for) the nation (if needed)
- be loyal to the United States

54. How old do citizens have to be to vote for President?*

- eighteen (18) and older

55. What are two ways that Americans can participate in their democracy?

- vote
- join a political party
- help with a campaign
- join a civic group
- join a community group
- give an elected official your opinion on an issue
- call Senators and Representatives
- publicly support or oppose an issue or policy
- run for office write to a newspaper

56. When is the last day you can send in federal income tax forms?*

April 15

57. When must all men register for the Selective Service?

- at age eighteen (18)
- between eighteen (18) and twenty-six (26)

American History

A: Colonial Period and Independence

58. What is one reason colonists came to America?

- freedom
- political liberty
- religious freedom
- economic opportunity
- practice their religion
- escape persecution

59. Who lived in America before the Europeans arrived?

- American Indians
- Native Americans

60. What group of people was taken to America and sold as slaves?

- Africans
- people from Africa

61. Why did the colonists fight the British?

- because of high taxes ("taxation without representation")
- because the British army stayed in their - houses (boarding, quartering)
- because they didn't have self-government

62. Who wrote the Declaration of Independence?

(Thomas) Jefferson

63. When was the Declaration of Independence adopted?

July 4, 1776

64. There were 13 original states. Name three.

Connecticut	New York
Delaware	North Carolina
Georgia	Pennsylvania
Massachusetts	Rhode Island
Maryland	South Carolina
New Hampshire	Virginia
New Jersey	

65. What happened at the Constitutional Convention?

- The Constitution was written.
- The Founding Fathers wrote the Constitution.

66. When was the Constitution written?

1787

67. The Federalist Papers supported the passage of the U.S. Constitution. Name one of the writers.

- (James) Madison
- (Alexander) Hamilton
- (John) Jay
- Publius

68. What is one thing Benjamin Franklin is famous for?

- being a U.S. diplomat
- the oldest member of the Constitutional Convention
- first Postmaster General of the United States
- writer of "Poor Richard's Almanac"
- started the first free libraries

69. Who is the "Father of Our Country"?

(George) Washington

70. Who was the first President?*

(George) Washington

B: 1800s

71. What territory did the United States buy from France in 1803?

- the Louisiana Territory
- Louisiana

72. Name one war fought by the United States in the 1800s.

- War of 1812
- Mexican-American War
- Civil War
- Spanish-American War

73. Name the U.S. war between the North and the South.

- the Civil War
- the War between the States

74. Name one problem that led to the Civil War.

- slavery
- economic reasons
- states' rights

75. What was one important thing that Abraham Lincoln did?*

- freed the slaves (Emancipation Proclamation)
- saved (or preserved) the Union
- led the United States during the Civil War

76. What did the Emancipation Proclamation do?

- freed the slaves
- freed slaves in the Confederacy
- freed slaves in the Confederate states
- freed slaves in most Southern states

77. What did Susan B. Anthony do?

- fought for women's rights
- fought for civil rights

C: Recent American History and Other Important Historical Information

78. Name one war fought by the United States in the 1900s.*

- World War I
- World War II
- Korean War
- Vietnam War
- (Persian) Gulf War

79. Who was President during World War I?

(Woodrow) Wilson

80. Who was President during the Great Depression and World War II?

(Franklin) Roosevelt

81. Who did the United States fight in World War II?

Japan, Germany, and Italy

82. Before he was President, Eisenhower was a general. What war was he in?

World War II

83. During the Cold War, what was the main concern of the United States?

Communism

84. What movement tried to end racial discrimination?

civil rights (movement)

85. What did Martin Luther King, Jr. do?*

- fought for civil rights
- worked for equality for all Americans

86. What major event happened on September 11, 2001, in the United States?

- Terrorists attacked the United States.

87. Name one American Indian tribe in the United States.

[USCIS Officers will be supplied with a list of federally recognized American Indian tribes.]

Apache	Inuit
Arawak	Iroquois
Blackfeet	Lakota
Cherokee	Mohegan
Cheyenne	Navajo
Chippewa	Oneida
Choctaw	Pueblo
Creek	Seminole
Crow	Shawnee
Hopi	Sioux
Huron	Teton

Integrated Civics

A: Geography

88. Name one of the two longest rivers in the United States.

- Missouri (River)
- Mississippi (River)

89. What ocean is on the West Coast of the United States?

Pacific (Ocean)

90. What ocean is on the East Coast of the United States?

Atlantic (Ocean)

91. Name one U.S. territory.

- Puerto Rico
- U.S. Virgin Islands
- American Samoa
- Northern Mariana Islands
- Guam

92. Name one state that borders Canada.

Alaska	New York
Idaho	North Dakota
Maine	Ohio
Michigan	Pennsylvania
Minnesota	Vermont
Montana	Washington
New Hampshire	

93. Name one state that borders Mexico.

- Arizona
- California
- New Mexico
- Texas

94. What is the capital of the United States?*

Washington, D.C.

95. Where is the Statue of Liberty?*

- New York (Harbor)
- Liberty Island

[Also correct are "New Jersey", "near New York City", and "on the Hudson (River)".]

B: Symbols

96. Why does the flag have 13 stripes?

- because there were 13 original colonies
- because the stripes represent the original colonies

97. Why does the flag have 50 stars?*

- because there is one star for each state
- because each star represents a state
- because there are 50 states

98. What is the name of the national anthem?

The Star-Spangled Banner

C: Holidays

99. When do we celebrate Independence Day?*

July 4

100. Name two national U.S. holidays.

New Year's Day

Martin Luther King, Jr. Day

Presidents' Day

Memorial Day

Independence Day

Labor Day

Columbus Day

Veterans Day

Thanksgiving

Christmas

English

65/20

*If you are 65 years old or older and have been a legal permanent resident of the United States for 20 or more years, you only need to know the questions that have been marked with an asterisk. (*)

They are also listed below.
Questions: #6, 11, 13, 17, 20, 27, 28, 44, 45, 49, 54, 56, 70, 75, 78, 85, 94, 95, 97, 99

"65/20"

People who are 65 years old (or older) and have been permanent residents for 20 years (or more) do not need to know all 100 questions. You only need to know the answers to the 20 questions in this section.

6. What is one right or freedom from the First Amendment?*

- speech
- religion
- assembly
- press
- petition the government

11. What is the economic system in the United States?*

- capitalist economy
- market economy

13. Name one branch or part of the government.*

- Congress (or legislative)
- President (or executive)
- the courts (or judicial)

17. What are the two parts of the U.S. Congress?*

the Senate and House (of Representatives)

20. Who is one of your state's U.S. Senators now?*

Answers will be different for each state. [District of Columbia residents and residents of U.S. territories should answer that D.C. (or the territory where the applicant lives) has no U.S. Senators.]

27. In what month do we vote for President?*

November

28. What is the name of the President of the United States now?*

- Barack Obama
- Obama

44. What is the capital of your state?*

Answers will be different by state. See page 48. [District of Columbia residents should answer that D.C. is not a state and does not have a capital. Residents of U.S. territories should name the capital of the territory.]

45. What are the two major political parties in the United States?*

Democratic and Republican

49. What is one responsibility that is only for United States citizens?*

- serve on a jury
- vote in a federal election
- the flag

54. How old do citizens have to be to vote for President?*

eighteen (18) and older

56. When is the last day you can send in federal income tax forms?*

April 15

70. Who was the first President?*

(George) Washington

75. What was one important thing that Abraham Lincoln did?*

- freed the slaves (Emancipation Proclamation)
- saved (or preserved) the Union
- led the United States during the Civil War

78. Name one war fought by the United States in the 1900s.*

- World War I
- World War II
- Korean War
- Vietnam War
- (Persian) Gulf War

85. What did Martin Luther King, Jr. do?*

- fought for civil rights
- worked for equality for all Americans

94. What is the capital of the United States?*

Washington, D.C.

95. Where is the Statue of Liberty?*

- New York (Harbor)
- Liberty Island

[Also acceptable are New Jersey, near New York City, and on the Hudson (River).]

97. Why does the flag have 50 stars?*

- because there is one star for each state
- because each star represents a state
- because there are 50 states

99. When do we celebrate Independence Day?*

July 4

Reading Vocabulary (USCIS Recommended)

Reading Vocabulary (USCIS List)

Your reading test will be 1-3 sentences. You must read one (1) of three (3) sentences correctly to show that you read English. The USCIS (INS) does not tell the words they use on the reading test. These are the words the USCIS recommends as the basic vocabulary that you should know, but there may be other words to read on the test, too.

Question Words	Other
how	a
what	for
when	here
where	in
why	of
who	on
the	
to	
we	

Verbs	Other (content)
can	colors
come	dollar bill
do/does	first
elects	largest
have/has	many
be/is/are/was	most
lives/lived	north

Verbs

meet
name
pay
vote
want

Other (content)

one
people
second
south

People

George Washington
Abraham Lincoln

Places

America
United States
U.S.

Civics

American flag
Bill of Rights
capital
citizen
city
Congress
country
Father of Our Country
government
President
right
Senators
state/states
White House

Holidays

Presidents' Day
Memorial Day
Flag Day
Independence Day
Labor Day
Columbus Day
Thanksgiving

Writing Vocabulary (USCIS Recommended)

Writing Vocabulary (USCIS Recommended List)

You will be read 1-3 short sentences and asked to write them. You must write one (1) out of three (3) sentences correctly. The USCIS (INS) does not tell the words they use on the writing test. These are the words they recommend as the basic vocabulary that you should know, but there may be other words to write on the test, too.

Months

February
September
May
October
June
November
July

People

Adams
Lincoln
Washington

Civics

American Indian
capital
citizens
Civil War
Congress
Father of Our Country
flag
free
freedom of speech
President
right
Senators
state/states
White House

Holidays

Presidents' Day
Columbus Day
Thanksgiving
Flag Day

Labor Day
Memorial Day
Independence Day

Places

Alaska
California
Canada
Delaware
Mexico
New York City
Washington, D.C.
United States

Verbs

be/is/was
can
come
elect
have/has
lives/lived
meets
pay
vote
want

Other (content)

blue
dollar bill
fifty / 50
first
largest
most
north
one

Other

one hundred/ 100
people
red
second
south
taxes
white

Other (Function)

and	of
during	on
for	the
here	to
in	we

For More Information

For More Information

Federal Departments and Agencies

如果您不確定該向哪個部門詢問，請先打電話到
If you don't know where to call, start with
1-800-FED-INFO (或 1-800-333-4636)
來詢問該找哪個部門。有聽力障礙者可打電話到
1-800-326-2996。

以獲取有關聯邦部門和單位的一般資訊。教育部
The U.S. government also has a website:
http://www.USA.gov

美國公民及移民服務局 **(USCIS)**
United States Citizenship and Immigration Services
電話 : **1-800-375-5283**
聽力障礙者，請撥 : **1-800-767-1833**
http://www.uscis.gov

國稅局 **(IRS)**
Internal Revenue Service
電話 : **1-800-829-1040**
聽力障礙者，請撥 : **1-800-829-4059**
http://www.irs.gov

美國移民及海關執法局
U.S. Immigration and Customs Enforcement (ICE)
http://www.ice.gov

兵役登記制度 (SSS)
Selective Service System
Registration Information Office
(登記資訊辦事處)
PO Box 94638
Palatine, IL 60094-4638
電話：847-688-6888
聽力障礙者，請撥：847-688-2567
http://www.sss.gov

社會安全局 (SSA)
Social Security Administration
Office of Public Inquiries
6401 Security Boulevard
Baltimore, MD 21235
電話：1-800-772-1213
聽力障礙者，請撥：1-800-325-0778
http://www.socialsecurity.gov

教育部 (ED)
U.S. Department of Education (ED)
400 Maryland Avenue SW
Washington, DC 20202
電話：1-800-872-5327
聽力障礙者，請撥：1-800-437-0833
http://www.ed.gov

國土安全部 (DHS)
Department of Homeland Security
Washington, DC 20528
http://www.dhs.gov

國務院 (DOS)
U.S. Department of State
2201 C Street NW
Washington, DC 20520
電話 : 202-647-4000
http://www.state.gov

美國海關及邊境保護局 (CBP)
U.S. Customs and Border Protection
電話: 202-354-1000
http://www.cbp.gov

平等雇用機會委員會 (EEOC)
U.S. Equal Employment Opportunity Commission
1801 L Street NW
Washington, DC 20507
電話 : 1-800-669-4000
聽力障礙者，請撥 : 1-800-669-6820
http://www.eeoc.gov

健康與人類服務部 (HHS)
U.S. Department of Health and Human Services
200 Independence Avenue SW
Washington, DC 20201
電話 : 1-877-696-6775
http://www.hhs.gov

住宅與都市發展部 (HUD)

U.S. Department of Housing and Urban Development
451 7th Street SW
Washington, DC 20410
電話：202-708-1112
聽力障礙者，請撥：202-708-1455
http://www.hud.gov

司法部 (DOJ)

U.S. Department of Justice
950 Pennsylvania Avenue NW
Washington, DC 20530-0001
電話：202-514-2000
http://www.usdoj.gov

更多資訊:

請蒞臨的網站 http://www.uscis.gov

也请访问网站 http://www.welcometousa.gov
www.welcomeesl.com

若要取得"美國公民及移民服務局"(USCIS)
的表格，請致電 1-800-870-3676 或參考
USCIS的網站。

CPSIA information can be obtained at www.ICGtesting.com
Printed in the USA
LVOW081711230513

335256LV00006B/611/P

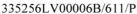